ISBN-13:979-8575748267

Cover design by: Samuel E. Dixon
Library of Congress Control Number 2018675309
Printed in the United States of America

This book is dedicated with love, hope and prayer to my seeds. To Michael, Nyiesha, Salea, Kareem, Amari, Zharia, Anthony, Aubri, Rhaegan, Amir, Truth and Morgan. I love you all, forever.

CONTENTS

PREFACE

INTRODUCTION

FIRST SEED - Responsibility

SECOND SEED - Distractions

THIRD SEED - Influences

FOURTH SEED - Roles

FIFTH SEED - Lessons

SIXTH SEED - Rites

SEVENTH SEED - Community

EIGHTH SEED - Facilities

NINTH SEED - Programs

TENTH SEED - Organizations

ELEVENTH SEED - Education

TWELTH SEED - Capital

THIRTEENTH SEED - Apprenticeship

FOURTEENTH SEED - Ubuntu

FINAL SEED - Action

THE SEEDS WITHOUT SOIL

NO FERTILE GROUNDS FOR CHILDREN OF COLOR

By: Samuel E. Dixon

Preface

As I put the proverbial pen to pad
contemplating what I would like to convey
through the words in this book, I find myself
battling inwardly about whether it should be
full of philosophical rhetoric to be discussed
and debated by scholars in the fields of human
behavior, sociology or anthropology and such
or simple language for all minds alike. I have
concluded that it should be as plain and
truthful as my heart and mind can muster. My
only wish is that some lives may be saved or
changed for the better because these words
have reached the ears or mind of someone who
needs them.
This book is for everyone and anyone, but
especially those who can identify with being a
person of color. The people of color that are
now or ever have been in the possession of
dreams, promise, and potential but found no
place to plant them and no one to lead you to
the fertile soils where dreams come true.

Introduction

The Seeds without Soil

It was 1966 in one of the many poor urban communities in the U.S.A., on a cold and gloomy wet winter afternoon with icy roads and whistling frigid air, a little boy was born to Gina; a poor teenage unwedded girl, that had no idea what motherhood entailed. With poverty the norm for her, even before this happened this girl wasn't sure who or what she was going to be, but now on top of being young and poor, her bad choices had forced her into motherhood before her time. Though she had, like other teens with unplanned pregnancies, considered abortion during the pregnancy, she could not bring herself to kill a child. So, she decided to keep her child without any idea of what she and the child's future would be like. After several doctors' visits, the child's sex was determined. It was a boy! Gina decided at that moment that his name would be Joseph because she had read somewhere that it meant "May God add/give increase". Though the young mother felt the excitement of carrying a life inside of her, during the pregnancy the young father was absent for the doctor appointments and eventually, the birth of Joseph. Soon after her problems began to multiply. Unable to work or complete high school and now having a child, she could only think about providing for him and having a place of her own. Living with her mother and step-father, she endured plenty of negativity and harsh words. She often heard things like, "where's his no-good father', or "we not

taking care of you and no baby too." So, an already bad situation only got worse for Gina. The father of her son was also a poor teenager without the means to support a child. He lived with his maternal aunt after losing his mother, only months before little Joseph was born. Both teens were in positions of need and unable to financially provide for their selves, let alone a newborn. Then, as if things for the two teenage parents couldn't get worse; Gina's stepfather ran the father away, saying that he had done enough damage to her and her future. Disheartened and hurt by the treatment she and her newborn's father received at the hands of her stepfather, she felt alone, unloved, and like a burden. Now, with all odds seemingly against her, she still knew that to be a mother meant she would need to take care of her child; even if alone. Flash to the present and this story or some variation of it has been repeated thousands of times, with more times than not, the same unfavorable results. A child growing up in a single-parent home, with a parent struggling to make ends meet and usually having to work more than one job to make it happen and that is only if the work is available. Not to mention that when the work was available, it was usually a low paying job, since most times the worker was unable to finish high school and get a higher education. Couple this with the unhealthy living conditions and environments that lower-income families are forced to live in with not being able to afford a better quality of life and you have a perfect recipe for dysfunction.
This situation fosters an environment where children grow up bombarded by outer influences daily, through music, television, and social

media as well as class-mates and friends. These children with their young and impressionable minds are hardly equipped with the mental fortitude to navigate and decipher the good from the bad or the beneficial from the detrimental. To an impressionable child, acceptance from their peers is the most important aspect of their social development, as we all have believed as children. In their defense, I would say that an empty toolbox is not a good place to start in completing any project; especially with the project being to become productive adults. Simply put, there are a higher risk and probability that children who have little to no support system at home and in their communities are more likely to succumb to these outer influences. Most people would readily blame the parent (single mother/father) for their bad decision making and having children outside of wedlock, by someone not ready to stand up as a father/mother or as a man/woman for that matter. Most times in the face of seemingly insurmountable odds, the single parent tries with all their efforts to support, teach, and nurture their seeds. Another problem, equally substantial lies with the parents that believe that they cannot provide the same unwavering support for their seed if they live apart from or are not in relations with the child's custodial parent. The truth of the matter is that by the time a child is old enough to recognize that there is a missing parent, they are old enough to see the absent parent's effort to be there or the lack thereof. Also, not to be discredited, there are plenty of parents that live with, raise and support their children financially, spiritually, and emotionally and their child still strays away

from the parent's teachings to be accepted by
their peers. Hence, the need for a non-
conventional support system for children
living in marginalized or poor communities,
who might face difficulties and challenges
often unseen by their peers or neighbors. This
is not an end-all or be-all solution to the
issue, but instead a shared observation of the
problems and ideas related to addressing those
problems.

FIRST SEEDS

Why are our seeds without soil and who is the blame?

First, let me point a finger at myself because my seeds have been directly affected by my lack of understanding as it relates to how to provide the necessary soil for my seed to flourish. To this day, I am still learning ways to provide the necessary soil for my seeds, through learning ways to teach them things that were not taught to me. With that said, we all as parents of what some like to call the lost generation must hold ourselves accountable for the part we play/played in their present perceptions, behaviors, and beliefs as it pertains to life in general. Let me be the first to say that "no one can be with their seeds twenty-four hours a day" and "I have taught my child right from wrong, but I can't be responsible for what they do when I am not with them". This is something that we can all agree on, however that does not let us off the hook for not providing soil for our seeds. An overarching theme of disparity and disenfranchisement is more than prevalent in most urban communities and most are living pay to pay or are one or two pays away from homelessness. This isn't right, and it isn't fair, but there is still hope, opportunity, and perseverance for our seeds when they are properly watered or tended. Just because a child grows up in a single-parent home does not mean that they are destined for failure. We have seen countless success stories from doctors, lawyers, teachers, judges, and so forth, that have overcome obstacles more devastating than what most children encounter today. Some were raised by grandparents, foster parents, extended family and some raised themselves, but they all can attest to someone pouring something positive into them. I realize that with the way our economy is set up (especially in urban communities) it is hard enough to keep the lights on and food on the table, so when a parent says they can't make a PTA meeting we all sympathize with that parent. However, we must at the same time realize that we cannot tell our seeds how important an education is without showing them that we support their matriculation more than just at graduations and other events. No, we can't always check homework every night, but it takes less than a minute to lay eyes on a child's notebook to see if they are completing their assignments. We don't all know today's school work as it has changed through the years, but paying attention to their completion of school assignments is still a relevant piece of their learning process. Not understanding their school work does not give any of us a pass to not show our interest in their education.

One of the major problems that we as parents of this so-called endangered generation fail to recognize is that we can tell our seeds that our present society is geared against them while forgetting to share with them that it was and is still geared against us. What I mean by that is this; the issues facing our seeds may be more dangerous and overpowering today, with social media, readily available synthetic and hard-core drugs, but we faced and still face major challenges as well. We can all attest to someone we may have grown up with or went to school with that is no longer alive and did not die from natural causes. So, we have more than just an idea of what our children are faced with overcoming. And as much as our children seem to want less interaction with us as they grow older, in most cases the truth of the matter is usually the opposite. Listening to our seeds and their thoughts about life, work, relationships, etc., can be the very thing that saves their lives, helps them discover their passions, and more importantly, allow them a safe place to just be heard. As we all know, there is no way to be of assistance to a person until we understand how we can assist them. Yes, we do have to provide a living for our seeds and a lot of us have no help at all in doing this, but we can lose the war if we keep our eyes on this one battle. We MUST make the time to talk with and to our children as they grow and have questions about real-life situations. Many of us have had most of our life's experiences as our only teacher about what life had in store for us. We don't have to let our seeds go through the same war unarmed. Every parent should equip our seeds with the necessary weapons to overcome the dangerous terrain known as school, friendships, relationships, and all of the other out-of-home community and institutional systems that they will have to encounter without a parent being present. One thing that we can probably all agree on is, that today's urban/inner-city youth or someone they know has an increasingly higher probability of drug addiction, prison sentences, teenage parenthood, and a slew of other negative life experiences, especially if they are left to their own devices. Since we were all teens at some point, we can relate to the parental/child disconnect, but our availability along with our and their accountability must go hand and hand. If we don't help our seeds understand how to handle real-life situations, in today's world, it could very well cost them their lives. Sad to say, but this is something that we are witnessing at rates that need not be mentioned. Still, there is hope for our seeds, if we take the necessary steps today to teach them the skills they will need, they can better tend their seeds in the future. Let us together, with our shovels of positive action and time investment begin to "turn the ground" to provide a better place for our seeds to grow. The harvest is plentiful, but the laborers are few.

Proverbs 22:6 Train up a child in the way he should go, even when he is old, he will not depart from it.

1 Timothy 5:8 But if anyone does not provide for his own, and especially for those of his household, he has denied the faith and is worse than an unbeliever.

SECOND SEED

Keep your eye on the brass ring; your neighbor is none of your concern. This world in which we live is designed not only to keep us from being compassionate toward our neighbor but to keep us from realizing our true purposes. It is not by mistake that we are taught that if we don't have educational degrees, get married to the perfect mate, buy a house, and have 2.5 kids, then, we are unsuccessful at what we were taught is called a good life. What we were not taught is that there will be almost 7 plus billion other people on the planet trying to achieve the same thing and that they would not mind pushing you down to get it. This is all a part of the plan put in place by those that consider themselves to be the elitist or more valuable people of this world. As long as they keep us believing that our neighbor is our enemy, then we won't focus on the foot that they keep on our necks. The enemy of our happiness and prosperity on the earth is as real as the air that we breathe and its only motivation is to keep us from reaching our true potential and purpose. Every living being on the planet has the same wants for their loved ones as every other being; this alone is one small example of all humans being more alike than different. The breakdown of our society began when the powers that be filled the minds of the masses with the belief that we are all different and our color, language, and ethnicity were things that meant we were not meant to live as one people. Lines were drawn and the earth was divided into imaginary lines that made people believe that their neighbor was not only different from them but

that they were competition. Minimize these
global lines and it becomes states, cities,
communities, and neighborhoods that have these
same faulty beliefs that were handed down
through the generations. Now a person is only
compassionate, empathetic, and helpful to
people that look like, speak like, and act
like them. This way of thinking created this I
and my attitude that took over and by default
made the self the most important thing to
everyone. Ask yourself this question; how can
we say that we want to live in a healthy
environment and only think about the happiness
of ourselves and our loved ones? The biggest
deception being played on us all is the
delusion of separation and it is more powerful
than ever with the invention of the internet
and social networking. People spend countless
hours looking at the images and words that
people put on the web to make themselves look
the best they can in the eyes of others. Then
that person, whether consciously or not,
begins to do self-evaluations of their own
lives, but with the images and words of other
people as their gauge. Not realizing that they
can never use someone else's measuring stick
to determine their level of success,
happiness, or fulfillment concerning life.
Just the idea that your success is based on
taught standards, ideals, and society's
measurements is an indication that there is a
chance that the false self is in charge of
that life. Which one of us can live completely
independent of all others on this planet,
without living in a world of lack and need;
either for material or companionship? It is my
firm belief that without an intentional shift
toward communal living, with surrogate
parenting, nurturing, educating, loving, and

inspiration, that our society will only
continue to propagate the delusion of
separation.
Without the educational system teaching
communal and critical thinking to solve the
world's issues, our world will never
experience the restoration and positive shift
in consciousness that it so desperately needs.
Our world has the technology to cure many
diseases, but the elitist would rather treat
people and keep people in subjection, with
their pharmaceuticals and doctors to maintain
their false superiority. What man does not
breathe, bleed, need sustenance, experience
pain, loss, life, and death? The false
superiority in the minds of men have created a
world that will kill people to harvest organs,
use aborted fetus' for experiments, video
record the abuses of their fellow man for
social media, separate children from their
families and do all these things with a clear
conscious. The selfishness of people today is
at an all-time high and the world sees nothing
wrong with this way of thinking. It is
believed that an honest person is a person
that is weak in this world and that that
person is a target for a crook that is viewed
as stronger. Humility is out the door and
nobody cares about anybody else's feelings or
well-being unless it is beneficial to them.
How can we as human beings come back from such
a deep hole of self-sabotage and detachment
from the answers, we have through each other?
Our future will be one where there are no
social service organizations, foster care
programs, social security or anything else put
in place to help people in need. There will be
no tolerance or acceptance for people who are
unable to acclimate to the rest of society or

to those who determine how this so-called society will be conducted. What will happen to these massive amounts of people that don't make the proverbial grade you might ask? Think of the people that are seen as the undesirables of the world today and how much sickness, despair, and hopelessness are associated with the people in those regions of the world. We have turned a blind eye to the sufferings of this world because we have been thrown into a state of dependence on the powers that be and to go against the flow could mean ultimate destruction and total ostracism for not only the self but for the family of the self as well. Who will stand for us all, if our education system is in place to teach conformity, submission, and like-mindedness? If our seeds are taught that education is another word for the regurgitation of information then where are the next generation's great thinkers and inventors going to bloom. The mind of the person that may very well unite the world and cure all diseases could be in some educational institution having his/her individuality and critical thinking abilities diagnosed as ADHD and given medication to completely suppress his/her ability to grow intellectually. We have so many things in place specifically against individuality that we have completely forgotten our childhood aspirations and have become, for the most part, just more fish in the world's pond, swimming with and not against the current. No longer are children taught to dream, now they are taught to be realistic based on the reality imposed upon them by those that would stifle their dreams of individuality and humanitarianism. We are losing a fight that few of us even will admit

is taking place against our seeds daily.
Telling our seeds that they have to be two
times as smart and work two times as hard as
the seeds of those in positions of power, is
another way of not just telling them that they
aren't as important as others, but that we
have resigned from trying to change their
circumstances. Why should we accept or expect
our seeds to accept the second-class existence
that society is attempting to impose on us
all? They look to us for answers and we give
them the same old, "that's just how it is",
nonsense that just perpetuates an already
negative thought pattern that they have to
overcome just to survive in today's society.
Unless we are ready to be awakened and to stay
awake, we will never be able to provide the
fertile ground that our seeds will need to
level the global playing field. They deserve
better than what they are being offered and it
is up to us to be the encouragement, support,
and inspiration for them to not only be agents
of change but to remind them what their
responsibilities will be to the seeds that
follow them. The proverbial dropped ball needs
to be picked back up and we need to put
ourselves and our seeds back into the game. If
we don't do this for them, then their ground
will forever be hard and will bear little to
no fruit for them and their seeds.

THIRD SEED

One of the first things that I believe needs to take place is to erase what I call the "Fresh Prince and Sprewell Syndrome", which a lot of the present-day generation suffers from. First, allow me to explain what the "Fresh Prince Syndrome" actually means. There was a 90's sitcom called The Fresh Prince of Belair, starring Will Smith as the main character. Will had maternal relatives that lived in an affluent neighborhood and his mother sent him there to live as a means to escape the troubles of his neighborhood and to clean up his act. Now, Will was a teenage boy that was from the inner-city who was street smart, well versed in the manipulative language, and leaps and bounds ahead in relational maturity in comparison to the children of his well-off aunt and uncle. As you could imagine, this made for an interesting storyline. Will, had little respect for education or authority, he had no real financial instruction, along with disregard for relational fidelity and yet he was portrayed as the popular, interesting character that lots of youth perceived as the person to imitate. On the other hand, and in contrast to Will, was his cousin Carlton. Carlton had a love for education, honored the opposite sex, was well educated in the workings of finances, but lacked the social charisma that Will displayed. Long story short, Will was portrayed as the popular, more interesting character while Carlton was portrayed as the nerdy wallflower cousin that wanted to be more like Will. The biggest problem with this portrayal is that the targeted audience (largely impressionable youth of African descent) bought into the idea that Will was the more worthy of emulation between the two. This idea seems somewhat far-fetched until you take into consideration that shortly following the start of this particular "program" schools began to lower passing grades and youth started to believe that being educated was a thing unnecessary to be successful. What this sit-com did not convey was that the next ten years would look very different for these two characters, if they both continued on their current paths. Carlton would likely become successful in his endeavors, while Will would more times than not become an employee of someone like Carlton. Fast forward further to the present time and we see countless youth frowning on education and choosing to indulge in behaviors that would make them popular more than cultured, educated, and financially sound. Their desire for popularity and entertainment is blinding them to their enemy at the gates. There are systemic and institutional barriers specifically put into place to keep impoverished people in a state of hopelessness and this helps to perpetuate a fictitious dream of materialistically making it in this society. So, it's only a natural occurrence that countless youth reach for stardom through avenues other than education and/or hard work. There are so many youths that have no faith in learning because they are bombarded with images of people that have made millions without education and/or hard work. So, when we try and teach our seeds the importance of hard work we are met with resistance or disdain. We can all probably attest to how

often our seeds respond with remarks such as,
"I am going to be my boss." These youth rarely
understand the importance that education plays
in their overall success; especially in
business. Not having financial literacy and
business management skills is a disaster
waiting to happen. We have to be there to help
foster an environment where their dreams can
be achieved and never tell them that they are
unrealistic. However, teaching our seeds that
education is of great importance will only
have a substantial impact when can show its
relevance to their accomplishing their dreams
and then help them move towards that dream.
Today as in years past, our seeds are charged
with taking numerous standardized tests that
were created without their types of minds
being taken into consideration. Test that are
telling otherwise bright students that if they
have no "real" or "societal" comprehension of
things, they are irrelevant and that
intellectually they are less than. I firmly
believe that there are only two ways to change
the way that our seeds view education. One way
would be to work with the current educational
system to insist that new teaching and
learning strategies are implemented in the
public school system. The other way is to pour
some of the money that we pour into this
economy through consumerism into creating a
new school for the seeds of marginalized
communities. The first solution is one that
hasn't worked since the public-school system
first became integrated, yet we continue to
protest and plead for changes that never
occur. The second solution seems more
complicated, however, when you consider that
the people of these disenfranchised
communities are the largest consumers of goods

GLOBALLY, it appears more accomplishable. If we all could do without a lot of things that we are compelled to buy and don't need we all would have more disposable income and thereby be able to finance the change that we expect others to finance. What I mean is that if we expect the so-called elite to help us close the gap between the haves and the have-nots, then we are all truly kidding ourselves. There will never be a time when a wealthy person will want the same for your seed as they want for theirs and it's just that simple. If we want our seeds to ever be on an equal and equitable playing field, WE have to be the ones to provide that field. With that said, if we are not being diligent in changing the system to a place that our seeds are receiving systemic, institutional, and educational equity, then we must teach them a new way to adapt to what is placed before them or create a better place. We have to begin this by first being purposeful in our doing away with media, both the social and the auditory that helps to perpetuate the fallacy that more material gain is parallel to a life lived more fully. Also, by explaining and demonstrating to our seeds, that in many disenfranchised and impoverished communities, the desire to feel more successful than their neighbor places them in an unrealistic competition with those neighbors. This brings me to what I have been for several years calling the "Sprewell Effect". The best way to explain this term is to do it by giving an example of the effect in action. In 1992 there was a professional basketball player by the name of Latrell Sprewell, who played for the Golden State Warriors. In 1990 there were Cadillac rims that would spin as you drove the car and the basketball player decided to design a pair of basketball shoes with a miniature spinning rim on the shoes, hence the name Sprewell's. When the rims became popular, they had a cost of between 3000 and 5000 dollars for a set of four. It was said that the rims did not give your vehicle a better ride, but on the contrary, it would make your ride less comfortable. Anyway, people bought the rims for enormous amounts because when they drove their cars people would stop to watch their rims spinning. Now at about the same time, these rims were selling, Walmart decided to sell a hub cap at a cost of about 40 dollars, that would spin as you drove your car, but not as fluidly of course. Herein lies the example of the Sprewell effect that robs some people of what could be their way to financial stability. On the one hand, you have the person that spent 4000 dollars for rims that don't add to the comfort of his ride, but people stop to stare and the driver's desired response is achieved. On the other hand, you have the driver that spent 40 dollars for spinning hub caps that doesn't either add or take away from the comfort of his ride, yet this driver also achieves the desired response. Now the standers-by that witness both drivers will normally applaud the driver that spent 4000 dollars and ridicule the driver that spent 40 dollars. However, none of the bystanders understood that one driver spent 100 times less than the other, yet they both accomplished their desired responses. Take this example and apply it to the shopping habits of most people in low-income communities, who believe that expensive and quality are synonymous. Not to mention, the consumers that believe that because they wear expensive clothing it implies that they have an affluent lifestyle. Our seeds are being hoodwinked and bamboozled on every end by rappers, actors, and the like, to believe that being able to purchase expensive goods somehow makes them better than those that cannot afford them. If we don't teach our seeds that driving a Mercedes-Benz does not make them a Mercedes-Benz, then the cycle of financial mismanagement will continue to rob our communities of millions that would otherwise raise the economic power of these communities. Our seeds are not taught that there is a purposeful reason that there are no decent grocery stores in their communities, but plenty of franchised clothing stores, liquor, and corner stores. We have to teach them that it is to keep them from eating healthy at less cost while ensuring that their money leaves their communities and that alcohol is made readily available to help promote unfavorable behaviors and feelings of hopelessness. We cannot continue to allow our seeds to be blinded by the facade of designer clothing and accessories that make some of our seeds not want to attend schools for fear of feeling impoverished. The enemy at their gate needs to be exposed and defeated if we ever intend for our seeds to thrive and not just survive. This can be done if we lead by example by explaining and demonstrating our processes. What I mean by that, is to lead by example through collaborating with those who are conscious of what is happening throughout this country to people in low-income communities. Leading by example is what our seeds understand, not telling them what they need to do, while we continue to go about our lives as if we don't need to change ourselves. We cannot expect our seeds to buy into any idea or belief that we cannot show them that we have bought into and that it works for the betterment of our people as a whole. We can't act united when some sort of injustice happens to one of our seeds and then when the media decides that it has been covered enough, just go back to the everyday life of work and bills. Our seeds are pushing through metaphorical soil, crying out to be heard, believed in, and given the chance to be self-sufficient young men and women. Yet they are being walked on and stomped down by their oppressors at every turn and we as the producers of these seeds stand by idly and accept that this is just the way that things have always been and will always be. How long will we watch as our seeds fight for their place in a society that shuns, criminalizes, and systematically and institutionally castrates their hopes and dreams? We have within ourselves the means to change their world and create the soil for them to be planted and to bloom. Yes, we have responsibilities, bills, mortgages, and so forth, but aren't our seeds our greatest responsibility. They are our true legacies, not the forty years of work that we have given to some company or business. Our legacies are not the houses, cars, and land that we can leave to them after we are gone from this world. Our truest and noblest of gifts to leave behind to our seeds is a world where their hopes and aspirations are not being shot down or controlled by someone or something other than the ones that produced those seeds. We can and we must give them the necessary soil to grow into their fullest potentials. We must explain and teach our seeds about the ways that society is playing them for fools by constantly entertaining them and convincing them that they need things that have no real value. We must teach our seeds that they live in communities and not neighborhoods or ghettos, by becoming active participants in the provision of opportunities in those communities. Sadly, the longer we wait for something or someone outside of the producers of these seeds to give them what it is that they need to grow and reach their fullest potentials, the longer we will watch our seeds fall into hopelessness, despair, crime, poverty, and untimely deaths. No, it won't be easy, but it will be worth it. However, they are our seeds and they are our responsibility.

FOURTH SEED

Let the line be drawn as to which
responsibilities belong to whom. What I mean
to say is that the society in which we live
has subconsciously blurred our lines of not
only male and female roles but father and
mother roles. Yes, they are an undeserved
amount of single-parent homes in low economic
and disenfranchised communities, but that does
not mean that they have to continue to be
single-parent families. With that said, we
have to first understand the full spectrum of
the dynamics intentionally perpetrated to
implement this attack on the seeds of these
communities. In 1935, with the introduction of
the welfare system to assist mostly widowed
white women, black families were still
ineligible to receive full benefits. The
country was still in the separate but equal
doctrine adopted by the Supreme Court in 1896.
Fast forward to the early 1950s when the
introduction of the "man in the house" rule,
that meant that welfare workers were required
to perform unannounced visits in the homes of
blacks receiving benefits. If there was any
indication of the presence of a man in the
household, the benefits were discontinued and
the cases were closed. This did not happen in
the homes of whites receiving benefits at a
higher rate, who had almost all of the fathers
in the home. To many, of whom I agree with and
am a firm supporter, this was the initial
attack on the black family unit as a whole.
Today it is disheartening to say, that this
situation in predominately black communities
is almost commonplace, even where there is no
public assistance being received. We must take

into account that some situations are uncontrollable, with the alarming rate of young black incarcerations. Also, the lack of opportunity provided for the vast majority of these young men, who are most times without proper education or skills to be gainfully employed. In most of these situations where there is no substantial financial backing from the family, the usually unwed or teenaged mother seeks public assistance. When this happens the mother, if she is not of adult age has to apply for services with an adult legal guardian as a caretaker. During this process and interview, whether for a minor or an adult, the mother must produce the name of the child's father. Without the name of the child's father, the mother becomes ineligible for any benefits. Understanding this process, what happens next is one of the most pivotal points in the life of the three people involved, mom, dad, and child. Once the mom begins receiving benefits, the father is petitioned by the state to pay child support in most times a predetermined amount. Most times, if the father is gainfully employed, he sees this as an attack on his quality of life and not just supporting his child. Conversations are usually had about why the mom went to the state instead of allowing the father to pay voluntarily and without government intervention. Usually or an overwhelmingly large amount of the times this conversation does not go as planned for the non-custodial parent that is asked to pay support. Often the amount of assistance provided by the state, is more than the non-custodial parent can afford to pay monthly to the custodial parent. When this happens, something unfavorable usually follows that affects the relationship between mother, father, and child. The non-custodial parent most times becomes distant and has minimal to no further contact with the custodial parent. Thereby producing another seed that will likely grow up without the necessary support of two parents, whether sharing the household or not. Thankfully, this is not the only way that this type of story plays out. Sometimes and to the contrary, these moms and dads rear the seed together in the same household or become great co-parents, while living in separate households. I am a very strong advocate for the latter. In any event, there is a disconnect that happens most times when a seed is produced in a low-economic household or community. The gathering of family and resources in support of the expecting parents that occurred in earlier times is no longer the regular practice. Nowadays, the usual joy of parental expectation is suppressed by thoughts of future responsibilities and obligations. We CAN bring back the strength to our black families, be it single-parent homes, co-parenting situations, or extended families. Within our communities and families, we have the financial, social, and intellectual means to nurture all of our seeds and provide the fertile soil they will need to grow. It has to be a collective effort on all fronts for this change to ever come for our seeds. It is my honest opinion that the change to come has to be initiated by the man in the community coming to the realization, that no matter what, our seeds are not just our responsibilities, but they are supposed to be our priorities. Not to mention that some men have been forced out of their seed's life, or the custodial parent picked up and relocated without telling the non-custodial parent. These things and similar things happen more times than I care to mention. The question is, at what point is a non-custodial parent absolved of their responsibilities to their seeds, either financially or emotionally? My answer is a firm and unrelenting "NEVER"! With the number of adult seeds from single-parent, broken, or dysfunctional homes that endured too many unwarranted traumas as children, you would think that these adults would stop at nothing to prevent the same from happening to their seeds. It is a given that every situation is different, but what is important no matter the situation is exactly what is at stake, and that is our seeds. As an adult from a dysfunctional childhood home, regardless of the dysfunction, it should be evident that even the minimal "consistent" support that all children deserve can change the trajectory and narrative of a child's life forever. Also, I would mention that the numbers are rising in male custodial parents, but as a whole, men in black communities have not fully accepted responsibility for the of our seeds. Thinking that "I turned out okay without a father", is not an excuse to be sporadically invested in the life of your seeds. No matter what age a man is at this moment if he is from a home without his dad when asked if he believed his life would be different and/or even better had his father been active and consistent in his life, the overwhelming answer is always a definitive "yes". Knowing this to be true for the majority of men in black communities, we need to be the ones to change the narrative for our seeds, not some government agency or politician. It seems to me that when there are no more governments or politicians to complain to or petition for help, only then will we understand that all we have is one another. We are a people of many talents, scholastically, vocationally, and philosophically, but we are an intentionally fragmented people. We are the answers to our seeds lack in this world, not the government, not the politicians, the board of education, or any system or institution built with our exclusion in mind. Our ancestral history and wisdom are far older than that of this Present Day Babylon we find ourselves in today. We are so much more than possible.

Fifth Seed

The lessons that were taught to our parents and grandparents are being lost without a real fight to pass those lessons on to our seeds. There were solid morals, values, and principles that helped our fore-parents to be people of integrity and character. Today our youngest of children is being commended for being able to navigate a mobile device before they can properly use bathroom facilities. Children are no longer being taught at home to say "thank you" or "yes sir and yes mam" and commended for how early they practiced this mannerism. Children are being raised to believe that selfishness is okay in the world outside of their homes, but not in the house. This is the easiest way to condition a young child into thinking that the people outside of their homes are in no way directly connected to them and that it is okay to not care about them. Compassion, empathy, community, and unity are all being lost and we are appearing to be willing witnesses to the death of the lessons that made those before us examples of great leaders, parents, scholars, and honest, humble, and hard-working people. Today there are so many of our people that are more than capable of not only teaching the things that better the lives of our seeds, but they are living examples of those teachings, demonstrating the truths of those lessons in their own lives. There was once a time where hearing the phrase, "I don't want you to make the same mistakes I made" was a normal thing to hear. Nowadays, it isn't rare to hear a parent saying, "they are going to have to learn the hard way". Both of these phrases are relevant and teachable phrases but better received by our seeds when they are used as one phrase, such as, "I don't want you to learn the hard way by making the mistakes I made". Either way, we know that if one of these phrases is uttered by a parent, that a seed has likely fallen onto the infertile ground. The question is what do we do to avoid this from happening in the first place, so these phrases are less likely to be uttered. Since every parent was once a child, I think we can begin to think about what it was that helped us become better or helped us become worse, when we were children. Remembering that we will not be there with our seeds through every encounter and interaction that they experience, we have to be diligent in reinforcing the words (morals, values, principles) that we instill in them on a regular and sometimes daily basis. To only teach seeds of color to be respectful to law enforcement and people of authority is teaching them that the principal is more important than the janitor, which isn't true. To not teach our seeds the important lessons that most of us who grew up with meager means learned about possessions and the value of things instead of people are doing them a major disservice. The simple things like keeping the things you have clean and kept were more important than having new things all the time. The way we were taught that what we had or did not have was not what gave us our self-worth was one of the most powerful lessons taught to earlier generations. The fact that our seeds today believe that their value and self-worth is being determined by the things they possess or anything outside of themselves is a clear indication that some of our most valuable lessons have been lost along the way. We are watching our seeds self-destruct without doing everything possible to throw them a real life-line. We need to teach them every day that they are being preyed upon in more ways than one and that their enemy is the most appealing deceiver. Lying to them by telling them that things will fill the emptiness of not feeling like enough or that having more than their neighbor makes them better than that neighbor. All lies perpetrated by their enemy come with false promises, but we have to be the ones to not only tell them these things but to demonstrate the truth of our words through example. Teaching them that respect costs nothing, but disrespect can cost everything. Teaching them that the adult in their presence may not be their parent, but they're likely someone's parent that deserves the respect that you would want their parent to receive. Teaching what I believe to be one of the most important lessons that the present generation should be learning, which is nothing on this planet has any real value to a person until that person decides to place a personal value on that person, place, or thing. We see this regularly through the simple observation of seeds of color and their economic support of things and people that add no tangible progress, personal growth, moral or intellectual enhancement, but instead gives a false sense of accomplishment and success. Instant gratification and a quick economic windfall ("come up"), has replaced the value of hard work, planning, and self-discipline. Doing the right thing for the sake of doing the right thing has been overtaken by a," what is doing the right all the time going to do for me, if the people I see get ahead is crooks?" mentality. We have to re-teach our seeds the importance of values like honesty, humility, loyalty, hard work, and integrity. If will continue to allow societal norms instead of sound moral teachings to be the go-to compass that our seeds look to while navigating present-day life, then they are heading to a place where their seeds will only further perpetuate the fallacy of the possession of things being equivalent to being of great human value to the world. We must be diligent in destroying this myth in the minds of our seeds or they as a whole will never truly learn to love themselves or others based on the simple fact that the life in a person is more valuable than the lifestyle or possessions of that person. Today more people are beginning to love and value themselves and things far more than they value other people. Without bringing back the value of another human being, there will continue to be a natural decline in empathy, compassion, and humility in our world. Of course, this is not something that will or can happen overnight, but if we don't start now, we are contributing to the demise of the seeds of our future both yours and mine. How would it feel to know that you're doing nothing to help our seeds today meant that their seeds and the seeds that follow will forever be in a condition of poverty and servitude because you chose not to act now? If you think that this sounds as if there is a state of emergency then you are right in what you think. The survival and ability to thrive for our seeds are not only at stake but it is being threatened at every turn and we see this throughout the evening news and social media daily. To simply ignore

what is happening to our seeds will not make
our hands clean of the atrocities that our
doing nothing will cause to negatively affect
their futures not only in this country but on
this planet. To continue to live as though our
responsibilities are only to our immediate
seeds and households while watching the future
of our seeds as a whole be viciously attacked
both systematically and physically is the act
of an extremely selfish or extremely cowardice
people of which I refuse to believe that we
belong. We shall overcome was a marching chant
for our elders during the civil rights era and
the remnants of those elders are people like
you and I that benefit from the sacrifices
that were made for us. Will we be the
generation that sacrifices nothing and
contributes nothing to the advancement of our
people in a society overtly and covertly
designed to stagnate any possibilities for our
seeds to have the substantial economic and
political advancement necessary for them to be
major players in this country. We have watched
marches and protests on our tv screens,
phones, and every other form of media, yet we
see no real impact or change that benefits all
people, especially our seeds. When and if you
overtly proclaim that our seeds alone are the
focus of anything that needs improvement,
change, addressing, or exposure you are likely
being seen as the enemy of the state, which
has to give you the indication that the
advancement or improvement of the conditions
of our seeds is contrary to the beliefs of the
state. How can we continue to not make the
changes that need to take place for our seeds
to thrive, while witnessing the dire need that
they are in at this present time? No one
person can do everything but everyone can do

something. The thinking that helping one of our sisters, brothers, family, relatives, or neighbors start a business, get a degree, buy a house or send their seed to college places us in a place beneath them in any way has to be destroyed from within. We are one no matter what our socio-economic, political, or professional status and we have shown this time and time again, yet we still have an overwhelming desire to be equal in a place never designed for that possibility. The biggest problem with that type of thinking is that the people that fight/march/protest for equality are convinced that any change in the right direction has to come from outside of themselves. The type of change that our seed needs to thrive in this society will not be readily handed over to them by their sworn opposition and to believe this is delusional. I am by no means saying that people that fight/march/protest for change are delusional, but what I am saying is this; How long will a person live in a dark house without electricity waiting for someone else to pay a bill that they have the money to pay? If this makes no sense to you then let me put it this way. People of African descent in this country are the world's biggest consumer of goods yet we are still pleading for help from a system designed to keep us in a state of need and servitude. We as a people have enough economic potential to implement whatever change that we fight/march/protest for ourselves if we understand that we are all we have in this country. I understand that there are people outside of our demographics that support this cause, however, I feel that always extending a hand to be lifted gives me one hand when I will need them both to push myself up.

Fragmentation is the destroyer of great change and impact. We must meet on common ground and raise each other on our shoulders one after the other, understanding that without the sacrifices of the few, the many will not thrive. I read a proverb that resonates with me and it says that "A society grows great when old men plant trees in whose shade they know they shall never sit." We must be willing to sacrifice for the advancement and continuation of our seeds. We must sacrifice!

SIXTH SEED

One way to ensure the probability of our seeds being successful is to teach them financial literacy, economics, and credit lessons along with morals, values, and principles. Don't expect their schools, friends, or other outside the home institutions to teach your child what we all know that they "really" need to know. It is my honest opinion that in the public-school system, the American history classes should be replaced with survival skills, which was a class when I was in junior high (middle) school. The classes should include the basics, like cooking, sewing, ironing, opening a bank account, and balancing a checkbook, and developing and managing credit. Some people may even remember taking a class called "home economics', while they were in school, but today we need those types of classes on steroids. So many students are going to high school without learning how to fill out a college/job application, open a bank account, tie a tie, or many other things that we assume that a young teen/pre-adult would have mastered by high school age. We see this all the time and blame the academic system for failing our seeds, but teaching them what they need is our responsibility, teaching them what the system wants them taught is the school's responsibility. Education in the public-school system is not true education by any means. In today's schools, our seeds are being taught that the regurgitation of information is equivalent to having an education. Free and critical thinking has been and is still frowned upon in the school system, where you are indoctrinated into the collective thought system of the non-elite masses. With this knowledge in our possession, to assume that our seeds are being taught what we know they need to know is us dropping the ball on giving them the necessary tools to navigate a capitalistic system. I understand that all seeds at all ages are not intellectually able to understand and retain the sometimes-complex processes that make up the economic system in which we find ourselves, but this is why we ensure that the process for our seeds is a gradual one. Even teaching them to save and plan for large purchases can be learned when young seeds begin to understand that money is a means of exchange for goods or that it's used to buy the things that they want. Either way, it all goes back to us teaching them what we know they're going to need to know to thrive in this society. Gradually we begin teaching more complex financial processes to our seeds until we believe or that they demonstrate the level of understanding necessary for them to competently manage their finances, without our guidance. But up to and before that point in their understanding, we should be diligent in our guidance and monitoring of their financial behaviors. How will we know when it is time to begin teaching our seeds certain skills some people may wonder, but when it comes to finances it can and should begin when money is first given to a seed. As early as that may be, there is still a learning opportunity presenting itself for your seed and it is up to us from that moment on how our seeds view money. Also, there can be the development and implementation of a ritual that is performed in your family that determines when the time is right to begin teaching and expecting sound

financial understanding and management. If a
seed is taught how to first understand what
money is, the types of money, and how money
works, they will have a higher probability of
being successful at managing their finances.
We are the people responsible for what our
seeds think about money and finances and the
earlier it starts the better their
understanding will be when the time comes for
them to need the information.
I want to speak a little more about the word
ritual as it relates to our culture here in
the U.S., as people of color. Let me start by
saying, we all know that our young female seed
is blessed to undergo a biological
transformation that can be viewed as a rite of
passage into a new more responsible age of
life. This biological transformation takes on
another less obvious path in our young male
seed counterpart and sometimes goes unnoticed
unless the change is accompanied by adverse
changes in behaviors. During this time, if at
no other time, our seeds need the sound wisdom
and guidance of their elders whether they are
biological or otherwise. The wisdom that is
shared during this period is usually only
based on the fact that our seeds' reproductive
systems have kicked into overdrive and the
possibility to reproduce may be discussed. At
this time, in addition to the reproductive
conversation, we should be having rites of
passage ceremonies however small or large they
may be, in which our seeds are accepted into a
group of other young pre-adult teens that are
being guided into adulthood by we the elders.
The responsibilities of being an adult should
be being taught to these seeds at this time.
Things like personal grooming and hygiene,
family leadership, household and personal

financial management (including clothing/grocery/household and personal needs shopping), vocational aspirations, physical attractions, and a whole plethora of other topics should be discussed during this time if it hasn't already taken place. If we are not discussing these things and helping our seeds understand that there is a process to everything that they could ever imagine doing, then they might believe the lie that their goals and dreams are unattainable. These conversations and moments of gentle nudging in one direction or the other can and most times do make the difference in the trajectory of a young person's life. I would encourage all in a position of experiential wisdom to aspiring to inspire before we expire because the future of our seeds depends on us.

SEVENTH SEED

Policing or monitoring our communities can and
should be accomplished by us and our neighbors
and would most likely be easier than it is for
the local police force. The reason that this
is likely true is that you and I have the two
advantages that they do not, which is living
in the community and knowing the people that
live in your community. Let me say that I hope
that this is your experience where you live
because society and technology have convinced
most people that there is no longer the need
for communities/villages anymore. Our
communities/neighborhoods are being overcome
by weeds (negative people/children) from an
untended field, that choke out the good seeds
(innocent people/children) that we are trying
to tend to fruitfulness. Of course, we are not
gun-toting police officers arresting the weeds
that sprout up to choke out the good seeds,
but we are the watchful eyes (farmers) that
are responsible for producing a fruitful
harvest. I know this language seems as though
it's getting a little agricultural, but I am
trying to convey a simple idea that I believe
is relevant to this topic. First, think of
every parent/adult as either a farmer or a
farm worker and every child as either a good
seed or a potentially crop tainting weed. Now
think of your community/neighborhood as
fertile ground for farming whatever seed we
wish to harvest and that that land has the
potential to also produce weeds. The farmer
that plans to reap a good harvest must tend
and sow his land to save the crop from being
choked out by weeds or producing too many
weeds, otherwise, his planting will have been

in vain. Remembering that when I speak of weeds (negative people/children) in this context, that no matter the current disposition it is still a seed, that is likely the fruit of another weed or parent that did not receive the proper tending or guidance as a young child. However, even with this being the likely situation we all find ourselves to be in, we must not lose sight of the fact that even the "weeds" are a part of our community. So, we have to find a way to use the valuable components of the weed without ultimately destroying it; creating compost of sorts, if you will. What I mean is that we are not to completely throw away those of our own, that through no doing of their own were subjected to unfavorable growing conditions as young seeds. There is so much good and potential in those children/youth though they may have been living as though negative and delinquent behavior is a natural part of their personality make-up. Somehow, we must show them their potential to produce the good fruit of their own through their becoming good fruit themselves. Through approaching these youth using the strengths perspective we can first draw attention away from what society says is wrong with them and focus attention on whatever strengths or gifts that they possess. Understanding that for some youth this approach will not only be different but not easily received by some because the support of any kind may be completely foreign for them. Still, we must turn a mirror to their good so they know that they are worthy of support and capable of greatness. We should keep in mind the difficulty experienced by any of us when asked to do a good job at things that we were not taught. I liken it to asking a fisherman

to grow a crop of fruit; unless he is taught
to farm, he will have a difficult time even
though if he covers a seed, something might
grow. After several efforts, the fisherman
might finally grow a good and fruitful crop,
but what is wrong with this picture is that
the unsuccessful crops are not vegetables but
people. With that being said, keep in mind
that in most urban communities there are
countless fishers, both men and women tasked
with being good farmers without the proper
training. So, we are tasked with helping our
fellow farmers (neighbors) to better keep and
tend their farms by offering assistance and
sharing the understanding and benefits of
communal farming. We are as a people capable
of figuratively turning the soil of our people
and producing greatness. Let's make being.
black great again. What I mean is that we as a
people financially support so many businesses,
companies, and people that contribute
absolutely nothing to the empowerment of our
communities or our people. We can create
programs that help to funnel our seeds into
opportunities instead of into the prison
pipeline. Of course, we have some seeds that
are doing things that they would rather not be
doing to support themselves, but how can we
ask them to stop living this way without
providing an alternative way for them to
support themselves. We are waiting for doors
to open for them instead of creating doors for
them to knock on that have people that look
like them standing behind those doors. Our
seeds are in a fight where we witness their
defeat regularly, only to look the other way
and accept it as what we have come to believe
to be our only fate in the land in which we
live. We may or may not be at present in the

position to buy land and start completely over as a people, but we are in the position to begin changing the trajectory and narrative of the seeds that we have brought into this world. We have to start doing something now or there will be no real tomorrows for our seeds to look forward to. How can we honestly say that we did all that we could to change the future for our seeds when absolutely nothing systemically or institutionally for them has gotten better because of our sacrifices. Maybe we don't have the time to sit on boards, sit in local government meetings, and protest regularly to help promote the change that we so desperately need for our seeds to have a level playing field, but we can do something. Every one of us may not have the time or finances to invest in a mass movement like this, but I refuse to believe that most of us want the world to buy that black lives matter when we as black people won't financially invest in programs to change these lives for the better. Of course, every person of color does not have an enormous amount of disposable funds sitting around waiting to be donated to a cause of their choosing, but we should not proclaim to care about the things that we are not willing to invest in financially. As the adage used to say, "put your money where your mouth is", if you believe in something. All of us have that one thing that we can do without, like having that small Starbucks coffee that some spend money on every day could be donated to the empowerment of our communities and the seeds therein. Sounds like not much to ask, but we are constantly throwing our seeds' futures away on things for which we have no real need. Then when someone brings it to our attention that creates an issue, because nobody can tell us what we need. Okay, I get that but think about how many of us go grocery shopping to stock the cabinets, refrigerator, and some of us a deep freezer too, only to stop for take-out food on the way to or from work or wherever. To be honest, most of us could be a bit more disciplined in our spending habits, especially me. The point I am trying to make is that we all can give something to programs that will help to empower our seeds and possibly create opportunities for them. If enough of us saw the importance of financially investing in the programs that are specifically designed to promote positive change in the lives and the narratives of the youth in our lower socioeconomic communities, we could make a huge impact. I believe that the sooner we as people of color understand that when another person of color is in a greater position in life than you are it does not mean that they are a greater person than you. Then we can better support those better suited to lead the charge and implement an impactful change and willing lift up and sacrifice for a greater good. The crab in a barrel mentality needs to be finally and forever put to rest if there is ever to be a chance for real and lasting impact and change in our people and our communities. We have to understand that supporting (African American) people of color has to be our priority and only when after unsuccessfully exhausting all efforts to purchase whatever product we need from someone of color do we spend with someone else. This is the practice of everyone else (even other people of color) but our people and we are suffering as a group while being so financially vested in the overall economy of this country. We have to learn to trust each other in business and support each other in business so that our businesses can flourish and produce more opportunities for people of color (African Americans). If a person seeks to be a better person and looks outside of themselves, they are grasping at straws and will find no lasting change because real and lasting change has to come from within. This fact is not only applicable to the individual but the whole when referencing people of color. The only true good for people of color (African American) is the good that is for all people of color. Love your neighbor as you love yourself. This does not mean to have a romantic love, but a family kind of love that wants for them what you want for you and yours. Treat your neighbors and their family as you would have them treat you and yours. We have within our own the ability to monitor, impact, create opportunity, and empower each other and our seeds. Remember, a house divided cannot stand.

EIGHTH SEED

How many of us live in neighborhoods without recreation centers or after school programs for our seeds to participate and socialize at. Likely all of us and the atrocity in that situation is that the taxes we pay keep the lights on and water running through those schools and recreation centers, that our seeds are unable to use. We have to get to a place where the local government can't give us a reason for our being unable to utilize these facilities to enhance the overall well-being of our seeds and ourselves. Within our communities, we have enough educated women and men to develop, create, and manage any type of program known to man, but we have to be unselfish in our sharing of these talents. We all have some no matter how little time that we can volunteer to help a child or another adult learn to read or become better readers. We can find time to work towards solution-driven activities in our communities, that may save the life of a young man or young lady. Even the adults will benefit from getting involved and many are interested in sharing what they know that could keep a young person off the streets and safe. The phrase "it takes a village," is more than relevant when we talk about what needs to happen in our communities. However, with our lack of stepping up and stepping in, our seeds are becoming more and more unapproachable and more disrespectful. I for one believe that we have within us the ability to save a large majority of those seeds and we should be throwing out life-lines every day. There are so many of these youth today that live in a state of "when in Rome do as the Romans do," who deep down wish there was a way out and a way to live what they believe to be a normal life. They should have that chance to live a life without ceilings on their accomplishments or their dreams. No seed of ours should ever entertain the thought that there is anything unattainable for them and their lives. It makes no sense for our seeds to suffer without us being willing to sacrifice for their suffering to end. They deserve so much more than we have been willing to give and I strongly believe that we want to give more and can give more. I only wish that we together can make an impact that has a ripple effect that grows into a movement so big that no one person can represent or be a spokesperson for it. Something that truly belongs to us all, you and your seeds and me and my seeds. As much as I am against asking any assistance of government agencies, programs, and the like, I would implore all hard-working tax-paying adults to charge their local councilmen to ensure that access to the public facilities that your taxes pay for are made accessible to the people of that community, after normal business hours. We should not be accepting no for an answer when asked if there are open recreation centers in our communities, while our seeds are dying in the streets for lack of a safe place outside of the home after school hours. Some if not most adult people of color can remember having recreation centers and neighborhood sports competitions that we and our parents were excited about attending and winning. A small thing like a neighborhood sports team and a group of adults supporting them can save countless lives from wasting away to the dangers that await them in our streets. We will hear from local authorities trying to convince us that there is no funding to staff and operate these facilities outside of normal business hours and that is when we have the opportunity to give to our seeds our most valuable asset, our time. We can volunteer our time, service, guidance, and protection to show them how important they are to us and our future. Our taxes keep the lights on and the water running, so we cannot allow them to say that we are unable to utilize the facilities. The next thing you will hear is that they are unable to ensure anyone there in the event of an accident; to which we respond that we will draw up simple liability waivers just like the ones we sign for our seeds to go on trips with school staff. They will try to deter us through all types of legal jargon and so on, but we have to remember what is at stake and that could be the life of your seed or mine. We can start by drawing up petitions to submit to the councilperson in each respective district where there are unused facilities and/or recreation centers available to the seeds that live in those communities. This being the initial battle of many to come when it has to do with enriching the life experience of our seed, we must prepare ourselves for opposition from both sides. For instance, the usual staff member at a public recreation center may or may not have a high school diploma, but they were trained in first aid and CPR and anyone charged with supervising our seeds should have the same certifications. The best thing about this is that I may not be certified or qualified to train and certify anyone, but within each community, there is someone that is qualified. It is all about identifying the human resources that are already in your communities, that are going to be utilized and seeking whatever pro bono services that they have to offer. This is so doable and it will only be as difficult as we believe it to be. The purpose must be greater than the person. The only thing that is keeping our seeds from achieving greatness is our commitment to providing the fertile ground for their growth. As much as I am for self-sufficiency and not asking for assistance from government agencies, they hold the keys to buildings that we should be using to advance this agenda. Keep in mind that this is not about the exclusion of people that are not people of color, but this is designed for people of color. With programs designed to target the deficiencies experienced in urban communities by seeds that only need fertile ground and tending to thrive and produce a fruitful harvest of their own someday, we must take the charge and create their so-called "promised land". This can be the place where they can freely share their goals, dreams, and aspirations and we can help them to start moving in the direction of those goals. Everyone should have a place to go where they feel encouraged and inspired to be whatever it is that they dream for themselves. It takes far less to help grow a good crop than it does to change a crop into something else mid-growth. What I mean is that it is a lot easier to guide a young person in a way that is fruitful, safe, and productive than it is to try re-train an older person that may be further along in their personal development stages. This is by no means saying that the older of the two is without the need for guidance of a fertile place to be inspired and grow, but that the younger mind is just more malleable. With that being said, whatever program or agency that gets developed must also be developed with the older seed in mind as well as the younger seed. There has to be a plan for those seeds that have been misled or not led at all and are in a place where hopelessness is prevalent. Our seed is addicted to a deadly lifestyle of street laws and thought processes that promote selfishness and disregard for human life, family, or community. These seeds have to want to live differently, be willing to work at reprogramming themselves, and be open to hearing and learning about seeing life and our world from a different perspective. I honestly believe that most of the wayward seeds do want to live a life where the worry of harm or prison is not a part of their daily thought process. They have been mentally conditioned to see life as a struggle because things weren't simply given to a lot of them or us and we have to help them change their perspective about what a successful or purposeful life is about. The self-worth and value systems of our seeds have been distorted for years and that needs to be a primary focus in the reprogramming of our young people. We all know that respect is something that the younger generation wants and respects above most things and they have proven that they are willing to die or kill for respect. If we can show them through example and demonstration how society is disrespecting their minds by leading them around like a carriage drawn by a horse chasing a carrot on a twig. Showing that the music, clothing, and entertainment industries are just that industries and that without their support financially these industries would not survive. So, the young minds must be conditioned to receive messages that are being sent or they would have to try something else to capture the attention and focus of young people of color. The young seeds need to know that there is a difference between black leaders and leading blacks. Our seeds are looking at athletes, musicians, and actors as the people to closely emulate instead of their parents, grandparents, extended family, teachers, or any other person that they are in regular contact with one way or another. I fully understand that these entertainers must do what they do to get followers, but at whose expense. The larger amount of the people that have our seeds attention are doing the complete opposite of the thing that will help them become better people while ensuring that their seeds are being afforded the proper education, morals, and values; at least according to what those that acquired wealth through the support their kind appear to believe. What I mean is that the entertainers that see people of color as their target audience rarely if ever willingly expose or promote their seeds to the mental materials that they freely and without discretion expose our seeds to. In my opinion, this is hypocrisy at its best. These types of entertainers are feeding our seeds garbage while feeding their seeds seven-course meals with dessert. We have to somehow clip the cords that bind our seeds to these web weavers of thoughts of low-self-esteem, body dysmorphia, materialism, and counterfeit opulence. These people that have our seeds throwing their financial security or chances for financial security away to be like, act like, look like, or be seen like someone they erroneously view as a role model. Somehow, we need to create a place or culture where the entertainers that are gaining the attention of our seeds are more concerned about the content that they expose our seeds to through their art, whatever form that it may be. Their art should do as all art is supposed to do and that is to enrich, inspire and/or provoke critical thinking; not plant thoughts of material acquisition, substance use, sexual promiscuity, violence, disrespect, and disregard for human life. They should not be comfortable producing art that helps in the corrupting of young seeds and we should not allow them to be comfortable acting as though censoring what our seeds hear or see is a responsibility that rests on us the guardian alone. They too have been programmed and this is why they believe that they hold no personal responsibility for any corrupted young mind that subscribed to the message or other things that they produce, market, or expose to young people of color. Therein lies a huge problem for us as a people. We must convince the people that our seeds are exposed to that they are also responsible, however indirectly it may be, for the information conveyed to young malleable minds, especially those of color. Some of us are trying unsuccessfully to instill communal thinking into our seeds, while they are fed a consistent diet of selfishness and self-indulgence through all forms of media. Today so many people of color are competing against their next-door neighbors to be viewed as the most successful, with a better yard, better car, better this or better that, all the while forgetting that as in the past to this present day, in the eyes of the so-called elite we all fit in the same pot; a pot that has been boiling over a lot more lately. We have to and we can change this way of thinking and create a place where people of color are not simply calling each other "brother" or "sister", but they are living out the true message behind our using these terms of endearment. When we begin to treat each other with the respect and consideration that we all want from others, then we are heading in the right direction. Let's start by being a person that has no problem with at the very least saying "hello, good morning, afternoon, or good evening," to other people of color without any judgment or reservations about that person. It is not much, but it is a good place to start.

NINTH SEED

Our world is getting smaller and smaller and our seeds are being placed in conditions that are counter-productive to their becoming upstanding and positive members in their communities. There has to be a way to create an environment for them to be able to reach their fullest potentials and where their talents are being recognized, acknowledged, and promoted. We can't continue to have our youth believing that a successful life means financial wealth because truth is told, few of us will reach financial wealth in this world. We have to teach them that wealth is a concept that is determined by the individual and that for many that concept does not require the acquisition of money or material things. Teaching a young mind to self-determine their concepts of wealth, value and success should be a priority for them to not become followers or conformists to whatever is trending at the time. Self-thought and individuality are becoming a thing rarely viewed in present society to the extent that when it is experienced it is seen as some other world trait or special gift bestowed upon a person. Getting in where you fit in is the flavor of the day and we are losing gifted people to this system of copy-cat expression. Our seeds are so gifted and so unlike any other that any trend, fad, fashion, or custom that they start is immediately copied, duplicated, and imitated. All the world pays attention to our youth for what the next hot thing, look or expression is, but we are the only people not benefiting from the fruits of our tree. The fragmentary thinking that keeps us competing with each other is creating fertile grounds through which every other ethnicity takes advantage of our creative and financial wealth. We must create collaborative organizations that foster an inviting environment for the innovative minds and ideas of our youth. Organizations must be created that also teach them the inner workings of a business, commerce, trade, marketing, and opportunity creation so that they are active participants in the creation of their futures. I believe that the easiest way to convince our youth that they are stronger united is by demonstration through our collaborations, where the purpose becomes greater than the person or individual entity. What I mean is that we are a people of many talents and gifts, but they are not being implemented in the most impactful ways. There are almost as many minority non-profit small businesses in any given urban community as there are probably liquor stores and corner stores in those communities. The actual creation of these entities for improving the community, family, and individual is more than needed and we can be grateful that many people are living a greater quality of life because of these organizations. However, if there is a community of people in need of services and there are competing forces/non-profits/entities attempting to provide the same service, the quality of service can only be as good as one entity can provide. Of course, that may suffice and the needed services will get provided, but if the competing forces combined their entities/organizations, the services would potentially and likely be provided more quickly with an improved quality of service

for all parties involved. Herein lies one of
our biggest dilemmas, which when brought to
the table for discussion can create division
because not everyone that talks about being of
service mean service to others. I say that to
make this point; if we share the common goals
of empowerment, enhancement of quality of
life, and positive mental health for people of
color, then the more united we stand the
greater our overall impact will be. We witness
the creation of mergers almost regularly
between huge companies that understand that no
matter how big they are when they are united,
they are harder to overtake. I don't have to
name names, but you know this to be true
yourself. If I am a small non-profit
organization that is providing a service in a
marginalized or disenfranchised community and
in the same community another non-profit is
providing these same services, I am by default
a competitor to that organization. Armed with
this understanding, it would only be in our
best interest to create a board and hopefully,
a larger organization, where the greater
impact can be accomplished and the probability
of the entity surviving and thriving will also
thereby increase. I am reminded of a short
phrase I recall reading somewhere that speaks
to this idea. To paraphrase it says,
(I)illness is what happens when we forget that
we're not alone and focus on the I, but
(We)wellness is what happens when forces and
people are joined in common causes and the
focus is on us. Our witnessing the unity of
every other people or ethnicity on the planet,
while we only come together when someone dies;
either by natural causes, taken by violence,
or innocently killed by law enforcement, is
almost like saying that we are content with

the state of our people as a whole. Now I am not foolish enough to say with a clear conscience that even close to a majority of us are content with what's happening to our seeds, but not enough is being done to stop or change things permanently. Hunger, homelessness, poverty, lack of opportunity, poor schools, inadequate housing, drug infestation, food deserts, bad water, and any number of other things make up the list of the issues of all lower socio-economical communities inhabited by people of color. Even with this being said, when you hear a person that has never experienced life first hand in these communities speak about what happens there, their attention is always placed on the crime rates. We the people of these communities know that they aren't mentioning how all the aforementioned listed issues of that community are the precipitating factors for the high rates of crime. Imagine yourself living in a place where the only way to survive was to live outside of what is thought to be the law of the land. Would you willingly surrender to your oppression or will you do whatever it takes for the survival of you and your family? I understand that what I am saying sounds like a scenario from a third world country, but for a lot of people of color and other people suffering from poverty, this is more than similar to a third world country. So, asking people to live completely upstanding law-abiding lives in a land where a large number of the laws are geared to keeping them oppressed, is like asking a person to keep their hand over a fire until you fill a bucket of water; it is senseless. Knowing the chance of getting what is due, deserved, and outright owed to people of color in this country is about as likely as the prison gate doors opening for people that are unable to pay bails on misdemeanor crimes. Being poor is a crime in this country and the worst thing about that being true is that is something that is systematically created by the people in positions of authority. This has been the way of this land since the founding of the first colonies that were built on the backs of people of color, both native and imported. I am not talking about anything that a child in elementary that has had their first American history lesson does not know. It is a strange thing how people of color are always told to pull themselves up by the bootstraps but have never been given the shoes or boots that were freely handed to immigrants that landed in the U.S. after the country was built on the backs of people of color? Yet to add insult to our injuries, we consistently carry signs of protest asking for help from a people that have shown us for hundreds of years that our lives will never have the same value that they place on their own and this in my opinion is some strange form of undocumented mental illness. It's seeking the approval of someone that understands that if they give you that approval their life will be drastically and negatively affected forever in countless ways that they would sooner die than allow to happen. Let's move on with those things being considered a given reality for people of color in the U.S... Instead of talking about the issues we were and are still being subjected to in a place where nobody has more literal skin in the game than our ancestors, let's talk about turning this thing around for our seeds so that it can come to an end with them. I believe that all lives matter, but I also

believe that our lives must matter more to us
than to anyone else, and then there won't be a
need to talk about our lives mattering,
especially to people that don't care.

TENTH SEED

Looking back to a time when the elders that came before us set down the blueprint through an example of how to get real change in the capitalistic country in which we live. Yet we insist on doing things that go against that blueprint today, even when we rarely if ever witness a real change as a result of those efforts. It is said that to repeat a behavior that yields negative results over and over, to get different results, is considered insanity. I would not be the person to call anyone crazy but to consistently ask for the assistance of people that has everything to lose if they give you what you ask of them is crazy thinking. We have to get our heads in the game and stop looking outside of ourselves to get the hand up that we people of color need when we have the power to do it ourselves. Without the change coming from within we would be putting ourselves even further into a perpetual cycle of dependency. We have already experienced a history-changing hand of help, like the one that took fathers out of the house for us in the past under the guise of help/assistance. Let's not forget to give thanks for the great hand of help that continues to give just enough to keep us dependent. We can change the game and the narrative for the seeds that will be here when we are gone by providing a place for the ones alive today to tend for the future seeds that will follow them. Though it is part of my character to live separately from people and things that mean no good thing to me, collectively many of us may feel a need to win the approval of our oppressor, rather the respect and approval of our seeds. In the end, the thing that we will be remembered for will not be how well we assimilated into a society that never saw us as equal but what we did to make a place for our people to live and grow. Standing on the shoulders of giants that sacrificed everything to give their seeds the narrative of a people worthy to be respected, the proverbial torch has been passed on. Those that came before us gave us the vehicle to move our people forward, but we sit our seeds in that vehicle without giving them the wheels or gas that they need to continue the journey. They are our everything and we must help them to see what type of people that they came from and how hard those people worked to give their seeds a place in this world. Not everyone had a stable home or family and to me, that is more not less of a reason to fight for those today that needs a place to grow and be nurtured. There is so much undeveloped potential headed to the cemetery and if we continue to stand by and do nothing then whether or not we chose to be, we are pallbearers by default. Our past and present actions or lack thereof are directly related to the demise of our seeds and the downward trajectory of their futures. We are watching the very minds that were created to not only save our people but possibly all of mankind, be programmed and destroyed by a false American dream. These creative minds both young and old that we as people of color have to draw from, alone in my opinion, puts us at an advantage in any arena we step into. They are the brightest, most talented, and gifts seeds that the earth has ever produced, yet we allow them and society convince that they are less than and the only way for them to succeed

is to work twice as hard as their oppressor.
This kind of advice given to a young mind by
default helps the oppressor of people of color
further their ideology of false supremacy. If
a young person is told such a thing, without
you having to say it literally, you have
indirectly told them that there was someone
better, more, or superior to them. Nothing
could be further from the truth and we have to
start pushing our seed to greatness. Our
people are some of the greatest minds on this
planet both past and present, but there is a
war going on for those minds and we have
allowed the enemy into our camps. The mental
programming taking place today is destructive,
corruptive, and most of all deadly to our
seeds of color. If we allow our seeds to
continue listening to, watch, and/or spend
time with or around the very things that
destroy their abilities to think critically
and individually, then we will get more of the
same. A lot of us are examples of what happens
when we decide not to listen to our elders, be
it our parent, their parent, or extended
family elders and we are the greatest examples
for our seeds. However, not enough of us are
in positions or have the platforms to share
the stories or experiences that could save the
lives of a young person or another adult.
Mental change usually happens through
programming or conditioning and we all have
been subjected to it since childhood and are
to this day experiencing much of the same.
There are too many examples to use but I will
just say that learned behaviors are one
example. We have to start using words like we,
us, and ours and stop using I, me, and mine to
begin to create the collective mind needed for
the change to happen. It sounds simple enough,

but the philosophy and psychology behind it
are sound and psycho-cybernetics speaks to
this very subject. We understand it as "if you
go to the barbershop enough, you will get a
haircut." It's not that hard a concept to wrap
your head around, just think of the way we
pick up sayings from our favorite music or
T.V. shows and it will make perfect sense. It
has been this way all of our lives, we are
just starting to pay attention to it. Music,
movies, and video games are real threats to
the healthy development of young minds and we
have to monitor the exposure that our young
seeds have to negative influences in the form
of entertainment. Frankly, it is the human
instinct of every parent or guardian of a seed
that their seed thrives, so what I'm talking
about is a human trait and not a learned
skill. At what point do we take a stand
against the so-called influencers that take no
care as to what it is they influence our young
minds to do, say, and think. I don't believe
that there any parents or guardians that are
not interested in the survival and thriving of
the young minds and lives to which they have
been blessed to rear. I believe that there are
no bad seeds, but inexperienced farmers
without the necessary tools to produce the
desired harvest. This is the reason that man
was not meant to exist alone but as a communal
being in conjunction and collaboration with
other people. Society is helping us
figuratively throw our seeds to the wind and
we are not giving this situation the attention
that it deserves. It's like watching your
house burn down with your babies still in it
and breaking out a bag of marshmallows and
taking your time to call the fire department.
That is how serious of an issue this is right

now. The excuse that we have to work is like saying that the people that came before us did not have to work and support us or our parents. It's a matter of what we are making a priority in our lives and the state of our seeds show that they are probably, for most, a close second on the list. Imagine that all of our children are literal seeds that we are responsible for producing a harvest from and within them is the potential of hundreds or thousands more trees, but only if it is properly provided the needed nutrients during its growing process. Now imagine this young seed being watered with soda and place under the shade of another tree where the light of the sunlight was unable to ever reach. In so many ways this is exactly what we are up against when it comes to providing a fertile ground for our seeds to not only survive but to thrive. Let's change the game, invest in our seeds, and not ask for help to come from outside of our own, when we are far more than capable of providing beyond the needs of our seeds. The question is and has always been, how important is the future of your people to you, or is your people only "your people?"

ELEVENTH SEED

What would it look like if you were the person
that decided what your child was being taught
in school, from elementary through high
school? The thought almost sounds like an
impossible thing for people of color, but
there are more than a few schools, where the
students are being taught the things that are
being recommended by the parents of those
students. The recommendations come along with
the funding and donations that pay the
salaries for the best teachers and staff to
create an environment of empowerment for their
seeds. The students at these particular
schools are being taught to critically think
and to explore their interests. This is
something that is more than lacking in most
public schools because the people in its
immediate community believe that they are
unable to be financially vested in their
schools and/or communities. The schools there
are staffed with mostly new teachers that have
little to no real experience with the culture
of most inner-city students and that is only
the beginning of the disconnect. This
disconnect is helping to add to the overly
represented children on ADHD medication being
children of color coming from mostly lower
socio-economic communities. The patience and
consideration that would likely otherwise be
extended to a student in a school where the
community and people are vested are not being
extended to the students in most inner-city
schools. The powers that be would much rather
label and medicate our seeds because that is
cheaper than investigating the precipitating
factors that usually contribute to a child not

be able to focus in class. Several things can be going on in the child's home, family, neighborhood, block, or even within the school to affect their level of concentration or participation. These are things we know about our seeds because either we are living in or have lived in these communities and may have personally experienced the issues that are affecting seeds today. With that being said and with most people of color experiencing the public-school system, we understand that our seeds need something that we didn't have when it comes to school, especially with today's demand in the workplace. The next question that I would like to pose is, who should provide the type of tailored education that children in inner-city schools need and deserve? If you said or think that the state or city where the school is located should be responsible, you are right and wrong. With the higher taxes being paid in most inner cities and less homeownership, you would expect that the larger part of those taxes would be focused on education, but that is not the case. If you live in an urban community then you know you pay higher rates of taxes for everything as well as car and life insurance. There is an intentional plan in place to keep people in the lower to the middle class from moving out of the lower class and remaining in the areas where they may live. An example would be a person living in any given inner-city neighborhood that pays higher taxes and prices for everything they purchase and then gets either a promotion or furthers their education, followed by a better job and decides to relocate to a surrounding county to pay far less for everything. This person understands that they will get more for their money just by changing where they live. This in itself should be illegal. A can of soup at a market in the city should cost the same amount as a can of soup in the county, but that is not the case and it's intentional. Armed with this knowledge numerous people prefer to do their grocery shopping outside of where they live and without even considering the impact on their communities. They are directly supporting an economy other than their own and helping to keep the prices low in that community. Yes, they are making a smart financial decision, but at the expense of taking money out of a community that is likely in need of more than is there already. This is just the tip of the iceberg when it comes to the correlation between financial, systemic, and institutional issues plaguing inner cities that we as people of color have allowed to take on lives of their own. The only saving grace about all of this is that we have within ourselves and each other the power to not only correct these issues, but to completely turn things around for our seeds. It is my firm belief that the aforementioned blueprint held the keys to restart this metaphorical vehicle of permanent change that we need. Let's take a look at what happened in the past and what results were achieved. First, allow me to add that I am by no means advocating for non-violent protests that result in physical abuse either received or given. In the past, any type of boycott that created a negative financial impact on the immediate economy of that place resulted in the desired change or definitive movement towards that change. The same can happen now with an even greater impact and additional benefits, with the use of social media, if we

do what's needed. We can reach the millions of
people that share the same experiences when it
comes to believing that our people's change
must come from within. Also, with apps like
"go fund me" and crowdsourcing, the money can
be raised to start making real change almost
immediately. I mean we have enough capital to
build our schools and industries if we can
stop worrying about who the boss will be or
why the person in another position makes
however much they get paid. We are all fruit
from the same tree. Just because the roots are
rarely if ever seen above ground doesn't
discount the fact that without them there can
be no tree to bear any fruit. This is the type
of thinking that is naturally communal and
understands the whole instead of the
individual alone. The individual is the most
important part of the collective in the fact
that there can be no collective without many
individuals collaborating and becoming a
single entity. There are several groups of
people of color that are starting up banks and
credit unions, where the focus is providing
the financial education and assistance not
readily available to people of color at other
banks and financial institutions. We should be
rallying towards these institutions, but we
appear to trust our oppressor more than
ourselves. We all know too many people that
have been denied home and auto loans by the
same bank that they have their payroll checks
going into every week or bi-weekly. These are
people that pay all of their bills and have
worked for one place and used the same banks
for years. We must honestly recognize that
there is an intentional barrier in place to
keep people of color from becoming home and
business owners and the best way to resolve

these issues is not to continue asking your oppressor for help but to look to other people that have experienced the same oppression. There are businesses and non-profit ideas that go without ever being created because it is not in the interest of what the "banks" consider a reasonable risk. The reason the risk is usually not worth it to them is that it doesn't further their interest in keeping people of color oppressed. It is my personal belief that in addition to creating banks we need to create charitable organizations where people of color are the biggest investors and the driving force behind the programs this organization develops and supports. The funding can be very small amounts that come from a large number of people and any and every problem that plagues urban communities of color can be properly addressed and eventually resolved. Opportunities can be created, after school programs, substance abuse treatment programs, educational programs, parenting programs, and so on, etc. The harvest is great but the workers are few. Are we going to wait for something that will never come and watch our seeds fall by the wayside because instead of attacking what is oppressing them, we remained passive at their expense? For the sake of simplicity, I will give you an example of how funding and a consistent flow of revenue funneling to the issues of people of color can be produced. Let's say that there is a community of 100 people and each week 50 of these people donate 1 dollar directly to a community organization in their community. With only half of the community donating 1 dollar each week, the annual budget for this organization is just 2600 dollars. This does not seem like a great

deal of money because of the scale of people
to money, but this is only an example of what
could be the answer to the lack of hope and
opportunity in our communities. Let's imagine
that the number of people is 50,000 instead of
50 people and the weekly donation amount is 2
dollars. The organization's annual budget is
increased to 5.2 million dollars and the
impact in those communities is far greater, of
course. The issue is getting people of color
to donate to a cause without seeing the
results beforehand and this is because of the
distrust of people in positions where there is
money involved. This goes back to my saying
that we have to start developing trust in each
other in business and financial matters
because there are astronomically more of us
with integrity than there are those of us
without it. Our distrust was and is inherent
in us because of our historical treatment in
this country, but that treatment did not come
at the hands of our people. Sad to say, but
the truth is that our people were better
towards each other as a people when we were
enslaved, because at least then we realized
that we had a clear opposition and a clear
ally. Today there are so many people of color
that choose to be any other ethnicity over
being a person of color or African descent
because of the stigmas and stereotypes
attached to being a "black" person. Today many
of us would rather trust their money in the
hands of a non-melanin having person before
they trusted a person that looks like
themselves. This is a huge problem and an
obstacle that unless it is addressed and
overcome no real and lasting change can happen
from within our people. When a person of color
is asked to give money to another person of

color there is a mental dialogue that usually takes place and it usually questions the integrity of the person receiving money. Take the same situation and ask a person of color to give money to a non-melanin-having person and the internal conversation goes differently and that's if it even takes place. Thinking and acting in this way, we have furthered the ideology and stereotypes that have been placed on us by people other than us and only we can change this narrative. However, we need to change it internally for self-empowerment, self-identity, and self-validation that cannot be given by anyone outside of ourselves. We do not need to change the ideologies or stereotypes that others have of our people, because what we think of ourselves will become self-evident. It is this form of low self-worth and self-hate that we must eradicate! Without seeing other people of color as people worthy of the benefit of the doubt before placing the same judgments on them as most non-melanin-having people do, it will be difficult to nearly impossible a task to get from where we are to a place of trusting each other. The trust factor from people of color towards other people of color is of utmost importance because only the financial collective of people of color will change our people's currently dire situation with lasting impact. I for one am not a racist by any shape, form, or fashion, but if I have to choose between giving my money to help people that look like myself to a person of color or someone else, the person of color gets my money. Without gaining trust in people of color concerning business and financial transactions, we as a people will continue to

struggle and wonder why our trajectory is
always horizontal instead of vertical.

TWELFTH SEED

How do we create this fantastical community or
place where people of color are caring for
each other's families, children, and
neighborhoods both physically and financially,
you ask? Through the creation of programs
headed by people that look like us know us and
know our seeds. We do not have to allow people
to tell us that the people overseeing the
mentoring and tutoring of our seeds have to
have this or that qualification. We want
people that care about our seeds to watch over
them and teach them the things that we want
them to know and learn. Bringing programs like
home economics and survival skills to our
seeds to give them the base daily living
skills they need to build on. We know that Ms.
Whatshername has been making clothes for her
family for years and Mr. I can't remember his
name has been repairing things in people's
houses in our neighborhoods for years and we
have these life experiences to draw from.
Countless talented people in our midst are un-
mined resources that would likely jump at the
chance to pass their wisdom on and will do it
for free. Let's not to mention Mr. Deacon,
that can grow an ear of corn on a 1 by 1-foot
piece of land that would happily teach our
seeds to grow plants, flowers, and more
importantly their foods. This is by no means
discounting the many gifted and educated
people within our communities that have not
just book knowledge, but life wisdom too.
There is nothing that we cannot accomplish,
create, build, teach, learn, or produce when
we are determined to make something happen.

When we work together there is nothing in our way and up to this day, the only thing that has stood in our way is ourselves. Not to get too scriptural, but the bible in Genesis 11:6 the verse says this," The Lord said, "If as one people speaking the same language, they have begun to do this, then nothing they plan to do will be impossible for them." I know some scholars and theologians will debate my understanding of the verse and discuss the issues of pride in man and that's fine. I am just pointing out that this is what was said before the Tower of Babel was destroyed and all languages divided. What I gather from the passage was God saying that when we as a people are on one accord that there is absolutely nothing that we cannot create or accomplish. Though every great change may have begun with the actions or ideology of one person, for that change to take place there had to be a gathering of people's minds, hearts, and hands. We all know that seeds of color are trying to find a place to blossom in a land where the fertile ground has not been created for them and if it does not happen by our hands then it will never happen. Remembering that we are the seeds of the seeds that withstood all that this Egypt could give and we are here to make their story a story of greatness. This doesn't mean that I am telling every person of color that they came from royalty and all that. What I mean is that we are a people that through all that has been dealt our way, we stand and continue to rise against all odds. Our seeds must be taught that their victories are our victories and the victories of those that came before them. Imagine being able to meet an ancestor that stepped through time to see where and what we had accomplished as a people, after having the freedom that so many died to have but never lived to see. The looks of happiness to see us as free people owning homes and land and so on would be short-lived when the selfishness, disrespect, and killing of each other was made known to them. Together is where we belong as a people and we look at having to live in neighborhoods where everyone looks like us as a bad place to live. It is never the house that is a bad place, it can only be the people living in that house. You only have to look at a person that makes less money than another person, but yet they live in a nicer house, drives a nicer car, to recognize this truth. The person making less money is just a better steward over what he has and that does not make him a better person, just a better steward. I am sure that most people have heard that people of color do not have a money problem, people of color have a money management problem. We must learn and teach each other and our seeds how to manage our finances and not only be a larger consumer group than we are producers and merchants of goods. The key to all that is needed as a people is to change individual thinking to collective thinking. This cannot and will not be done without people of color uniting in the areas that make people strong. We need to first start to allow our money to make money for us by creating financial institutions and/or supporting the ones already in existence that are run and owned by people of color. It has to be understood that doing business with your kind is not a form of counter-racism, but it is simply the best business practices. Every other ethnicity performs business in this same manner and they

are not being called racist for these
practices. After building a strong financial
institution, the funds can be generated to
build schools and other organizations that
promote the empowerment of people of color. If
a school is built by people of color for
people of color, then people of color are not
being racist by any means, but they are
joining in on what has been happening all
along. If there was a plan to educate our
seeds with what they needed to be as
successful as the seeds of their oppressors,
it would have happened by now. It is our job
and our job only. The crazy thing about this
fact is that the oppressor knows this, but
they also know that our selfishness won't
allow us to sacrifice our prestige or
recognition to uplift the whole of the group.
They have figuratively bet the farm on that
being a fact. Think about how every time there
is a leader of people of color that tries to
empower their people and teaches or exposes
them to the ways of their oppressor, something
happens to the person. Their names and
reputations are somehow slandered or they
become physically unable to continue in the
work of lifting their kind due to attacks or
assassination. We know this to be true of
almost anyone that stood up and spoke out
against their oppressor. What I am talking
about and or proposing has nothing to do with
communicating with the oppressor about the
things that they are already aware that they
are doing or have in place to keep people of
color stagnate. Also, I am not talking about
any covert organizing behind the backs of
anybody either, whether people of color or
otherwise. What I propose is to use the same
structural, financial, and institutional

systems model that is being used against people of color to empower people of color. By creating organizations and allowing the people that you want to sit on your boards you are not committing a crime, but using proper and best business etiquette. Many people come to the U.S. to get educated on a particular subject to take what they've learned back to their homes to better the quality of life for their people. When do we start using what we know to make the quality of life better for our people and want for our people what we want for our seeds and ourselves? I for one believe that this is more than possible, it is doable. This can be done in our lifetime if we start making the changes now. Let's make this a reality for our seeds.

THIRTEENTH SEED

Who will listen is the question I often ask myself when it comes to sharing ideas about what it takes to implement real change in our communities? It is my sincerest hope that someone will agree with the ideas that are shared, enough to initiate a positive change in their environment that becomes contagious and spreads like a pandemic. One of the ideas that I would like to share and see created where you are is what I like to call, "The Communal People Pool". This is a place where the people in any inner-city or lower socio-economic community creates a pool of people within their community that have different skill sets. Through a questionnaire or short survey, this neighborhood is combed to see just what type of tradesmen and professionals live in their area. Two of the main questions would ask if the persons, young or old would like to share pro-bono whatever trade or skill that they possess with the people of their community and would they be interested in attending free training. With the information gathered and skillsets categorized, the next thing would be to use the information from the survey to see how many people are interested in learning these skills to see what size place you will need. Next, and if there is no predetermined place readily available, reach out to the local public library and negotiate a time and space there to use as an area to do whatever training you want. I know that more dynamics will come into play, but things like this are inexpensive and doable. Another good thing about this type of endeavor is that it can help with getting the community on board

with helping each other and it can become a
foundation or non-profit. Using the funds, you
can then find available space to create a
community's space/hub for these types of
training, speaking engagements, community
gatherings and/or town hall meetings, etc.
Everything else can be developed from this
community hub, with the help and collaboration
of the people in the community. Again. there
will be other dynamics at play but as a
team/board of people with different skill
sets, things can be easily ironed out. This is
only one idea of the many hibernating in the
minds of our people and seeds and I am hoping
to help us get the conversations started about
ways to change the narrative of what we see
happening to our seeds and our people as a
whole. There are so many innovative ideas that
the young minds of people of color want to
share, but they have no place of their own to
plant those thoughts or ideas. We CAN create
these places for them! A place where they can
feel empowered, safe, encouraged, and inspired
to dream of greatness again and leave behind
feelings of hopelessness low self-worth.
Within our power, knowledge, and finances we
have more than what it takes to create
programs that teach our seeds how to raise
funds for business ideas, inventions, or
whatever their ideas may be, and creating this
place should be our priority. The lessons of
life, daily living, relational communications,
self-discipline, conflict resolution, and
other lessons that can help in our seeds
supporting themselves should be learned from
people like ourselves that look like them. Our
children are dying for nothing in these
streets and the police are not the only people
killing them. We are killing each other at a

rate that would create a national emergency if they were non-melanin-having people. They have no skills to even deal with each other and are being taught through music, so-called friends, and whatever other means that their brothers and sisters are their opposition. This is a badge that they are wearing proudly and we are standing by watching this happen, because of the fear of aggression from our seeds for interjecting and speaking the truth into their lives. These seeds do not have the necessary conflict resolution skills that will allow them to walk away from situations without killing or being killed for things that will later amount to absolutely nothing of significance. They live and die for the respect that they don't even know how to extend to themselves and they are dying at alarming rates to get this respect. Also, when these types of things happen in our communities, there is rarely to never any type of mental health professionals coming into these communities to ensure that the seeds there can process through a traumatic situation without being permanently scarred. In contrast, when a shooting takes place at different schools, especially those with a predominantly non-melanin-having population, mental health professionals are swarming the place. Our seeds need far more mental health counseling than probably any other population of seeds on the planet. We have to teach them that their lives are worth so much more than what they are allowing others to purchase and destroy them for and that we want them to live and have a chance. I believe that we have to be the ones to model the positive behaviors that we expect from them, by treating each other as we would like to be treated. For them

to consistently see that we do not extend
common respect to each other and that if
anything of value is at stake, we will throw
respect for others out of the situation is a
sad learning experience for our seeds. We can
and we must do better. We must stop allowing
this world to bury our futures in the
graveyard. Where is there promise land? Who
will fight for them? Where will they be
planted and bloom? Our seeds will be planted
and bloom where we provide the place for them
and only there!

FOURTEENTH SEED

Where are the places that we can start doing
what needs to be done for our seeds to grow
and have a legacy of love, family, and village
to pass on to future generations? First, we
have to realize that this type of movement has
to start with people that can discern whether
the persons that they are sharing their ideas
with is friend or foe. Many people will claim
to be on the side of empowering people of
color, but they have ulterior motives which
usually turn out to be either sabotage or
infiltration for outside sources. Not that the
organization should be a secret, but the
people that are charged with the day to day
operations have to be people of integrity.
There will be opposition coming from all sides
and the worst will probably come from other
people of color, but the purpose will be
greater than the persons. If our seeds will
ever have a real chance for equity in this
country, we will have to equip them with the
knowledge and skills that make them the most
desirable of candidates in all areas. We must
build a school for our seeds that resembles a
warehouse or production factory, where we are
solely invested in producing the world's best
seeds. This should be relatively simple since
these seeds are already the best, brightest,
and strongest. The strength of this seed has
been known since forever and even though there
have been attempts to weaken the potency of
the seed, it still holds its biological and
creative dominance compared to all other
seeds. We have to educate our children and
teach them what empowers them not that if they
are of African American descent that they

likely had ancestors that were enslaved. This type of education is only meant to create feelings of inferiority and reinforces that people of color are somehow non-indigenous to stolen land, where they mined, formed, and laid the cornerstones of its foundations. Without the strength, mental and physical fortitude of people of color there would be no country in North America for anyone outside of the indigenous Native Americans to claim as a country or collection of states. Also, if when the educational system was so proudly planting thoughts of inferiority in children of color, they were simultaneously teaching non-melanin having students that if they have a long family history in this country that they are likely the descendants of murdering rapist that killed unarmed people, bought captive humans and used them like they were animals to colonize a land that they had stolen from a peaceful people. This will not happen because they do not want their seeds to feel like they are the descendants of a people that have no conscience when it comes to the atrocities that they are willing to commit in the name of conquest, domination, and the right to rob people of color for land and resources for the benefit of their own. I don't want to say any more about what is not happening in public school systems, I would rather discuss ways to create the funds to build a school for seeds of color that will give them the knowledge that we want future generations to know. As I have said throughout this book, the funds have to come from us, if we want full control over what will be taught to our seeds. There are several ways to financially contribute to a cause like ours and an unsubstantial weekly or bi-weekly donation coming from enough like-

minded people of color is more than enough to
get the real change that is needed. When I say
unsubstantial, I mean that in the most literal
sense possible. I've said earlier and I am
saying this again that the amount of a
donation is not as important as the number of
donators. So the financial contribution should
in no way place any type of additional strain
on anyone that is struggling already. Our
programs will be geared to empowerment not
adding to the issues plaguing our communities.
I am doing what I can to create this type of
environment in the community where I grew up
and it can happen in every urban community
across this country, where people of color are
struggling to be villages. Let us never forget
the phrase, "I am because we are." I cannot
say enough about how important this mission is
to me and what it means for our seeds to have
a real chance to thrive in this land. I say
this land because if we continue to see this
country as a place where we are recognized as
natives, we will continue to be blinded to the
dependency we've allowed ourselves to fall
captive to in the beginning. If we begin to
see this country as a new land where we have
to make a place for our seeds then we begin to
have the right ideas about what it is that we
need to do for them. I know this sounds a
little non-conventional and some people of
color will say that with all the skin that our
ancestors have in the game that this our
country too, and I will not disagree. However,
what I will say is that the place in this
country that is ours will never be readily
handed over to us and unless we prepare the
figurative land and plant our seeds in the
fertile soil of our own making. To put it
bluntly, the powers that be in this country

have no real respect for us as a people. From the beginnings of our freedom in this country and the centuries of brainwashing it has always appeared to them that our people aspired to be them or at least like them, but inherently we are not like them. We are a different breed and we have taken on the ideals and habits of our oppressor, like a person leaving an abusive relationship but taking the behaviors of their abuser into their next relationship. We have to shake the dust from our captors off of our garments and sandals, so to speak or we will never walk our seeds into the promised land.

FINAL SEED

People always ask me what have I done to
implement change where I live, work, and have
my being. I always respond with the fact that
I have and continue to pour into young seeds
of color because I was a young seed with
places to thrive and did not take advantage of
my opportunity. I was a victim of my thinking
in addition to the physical and psychological
abuse I endured through words and actions, so
my views of a happy family are somewhat
tainted. Don't get me wrong, I was lucky that
my mom eventually dated a man that decided
that even though the three children weren't
his, he would stay. Only later in life did I
realize that my thoughts and actions as a
young adult were in direct relation to my home
life and the environment in which I lived.
Some people don't believe in the emotional and
mental effects that growing up in single-
parent and abusive homes has on the psyche of
young impressionable minds. People can readily
give examples of people that have overcome
seemingly insurmountable obstacles to become
successful, but two plants in the same soil,
side by side and watered the same don't always
grow the same. People are no different. We are
all individuals and what may be traumatic to
some may be normal to another. As for me, I
like many seeds that we encounter today, was
good at hiding the pain and disappointment
that I had in the parents that were supposed
to be my guides, protectors, and providers.
The hiding manifested itself in substance use
and then abuse, promiscuous sexual behaviors,
lack of respect for authority and self.
Without being taught that we are not our

circumstances, those circumstances have a high probability of harming us in ways that may only manifest themselves later in life. Almost every young seed that is in some kind of negative situation today has likely had a negative home experience and that is if some have even had a biological home experience. Even those that did not have what would be considered a negative home experience may have only been provided for physically and financially, but not emotionally and they never learned to process thoughts or to resolve conflicts. This lack of understanding of their thought processes can cause the impulsive behaviors that we see destroying our seeds today. Also, the lessons that they need to learn will not just drop out of the sky and into their heads, we have to teach them ourselves. What we see today is the result of years of untreated mental health disorders presenting through violence, abandonment, self-medicating, and an overall state of hopelessness. This is a public health issue that goes on unchecked as a crime or poverty issue that is plaguing communities with little to no opportunities readily available for its population. However, all the issues that result from these community problems being unaddressed are affecting the public's health in these areas and the surrounding areas. To witness the astronomical numbers of homicides in communities of color and continue to view this as only a problem stemming from issues related to poverty without understanding the mental state of the people committing the crimes. It's like having two parents with sickle cell anemia, knowing that it is hereditary, you begin showing signs of the disease, and the doctor checks you for high blood pressure. Most times in communities of color, violence, and hopelessness is a passed-on personality trait that young seeds without proper guidance and support systems can find themselves becoming victims to without realizing it. If we do not address and attack psychological cancer that is killing our seeds and destroying our families and communities, our seeds will continue on this downward spiral that is contributing to their feelings of hopelessness. I know that this sounds like a task that is nearly impossible, however with everything negative that has already transpired in our communities and the lives of our seeds, at the very least we should be collectively trying any and everything we can to change the narrative of their lives. The word us has to be re-introduced into the vocabulary of people in neighborhoods of color, starting with the people on our blocks. Also, we need to make sure that we continue to act in this way, instead of having the short-term emergences of outrage that happens when something happens to someone. The problem does not end when the marches or protests end and we have to continue to fuel the fight for our seeds to have their fair shots in this world, not just this country. The collective minds and hearts of people of color must be united to create the force that will be needed to make the change real and lasting. Programs need to be created now that provide opportunities for our seeds to have a place that promotes and highlights their gifts and helps to open doors for them to walk through. There is nothing too big for us as a people to accomplish together! Our cause is just and our fight is a valid one, so we will succeed, if we refuse to quit. Our seeds are more than

worth anything that we may have to sacrifice
to ensure that they have a future. When I was
a young seed, I was given opportunities that
do not exist today for our seeds and we don't
do something right now no opportunities will
be there for their seeds either. Things that
were taken for granted like recreation
centers, free lunches, sports, and summer camp
programs are things that have gradually
disappeared from the options list for our
seeds. Now we are tasked with recreating the
spaces and opportunities that our seeds will
need to thrive and I believe that we are up to
the job. There are countless youth today that
are without their parents' support or the
support of family, who need consistent real,
and lasting change that is transferable to the
seeds that they will parent. So many of us
never learned how to parent ourselves and some
of us have children now that have been
negatively affected by our lack of parenting
skills. They in turn have children that suffer
the same lack since their parents were not
taught either. The cycle has to end. We should
not be ashamed to apologize to our seeds for
not being equipped with what we needed to help
them be the parents that we weren't able to
be. We should be ashamed to continue allowing
this shortcoming to ravage our family
structures from generation to generation.
There is no shame in taking a parenting class
to be able to better teach your seeds how to
parent. Pride has kept us from approaching the
seeds that shun us because we abandoned them
at some point. And what's worst is that when
this happens, some parents are quick to use
the fact that no one taught them to parent as
a means of escaping their parental
responsibilities. Either way, I am speaking to

what has happened and not what needs to happen. Not only is it important for us to change the narrative and trajectories of their lives, but through our focus on their futures, we will also change our narratives. Let's stop competing with our neighbors, co-workers, other black organizations, friends, and for some of us even family members. There is no way that we will ever amount to or transcend into the great people that we are until we at first love each other as we love ourselves. They say that once you have learned a thing that you are forever a new or different person and that having new knowledge should somehow change you either negatively or positively. I am not sure if anything I shared was new for you, inspired you, angered you, or moved you to action, but I hope you were in some way inspired. As for me, I will continue to do my best at accepting, inspiring, empowering, helping, uplifting, sharing with, giving to, and serving every person that I encounter as long as I live this life, but first I will serve my own. Join me...